Fountain

Respect for Sources

James Stone Goodman

For my beloveds

Psalm 105
Sing it
Swing it
Talk about it

CONTENTS

SILENCE

LISTENING

MEMORY

PRACTICING

TEACHING

THANKFUL

Shaping the Book

I learned the figure below from the Spanish-Jewish poet Ibn Gabirol, 11th century, Andalusian. He was an accomplished poet though by many accounts he died before the age of 40. There is also a tradition that he wrote *Adon Olam*, a well known Jewish liturgical poem in Hebrew.

From another work attributed to him, *Mivchar ha-Peninim*/Choice of Pearls*, I brought down a guideline, a fragment, a pericope. *Choice of Pearls* is a compilation of ethical aphorisms, like the *Book of Proverbs* from the Hebrew Bible, and it is not certain that Ibn Gabirol wrote the *Choice of Pearls* at all.

He wrote this about acquiring wisdom:

Silence [*shtikah*]	שתיקה
Listening [*shmi'ah*]	שמיעה
Memory [*zikaron*]	זכרון
Practice [*ma'aseh*]	מעשה
Teaching [*moreh/morah*]	מורה
Thankful (in some versions) [*modeh/modah*]	מודה

It has stayed with me as a kind of guideline, like a workbook. When trying to learn something, when I don't know exactly what to do, I begin with silence, clearing out the space to encounter the world on its own terms.

What follows is listening. Here I am more attentive because I have begun in silence. I become more intentional by listening.

What follows is memory: To remember what I know. A reminder what I have been taught, what I know that I can apply to the problem or the subject or the challenge I am encountering. Remembering what my teachers, inspirations, influences, my

9

beloveds have planted within me that I can draw upon and apply to the challenge. What I have received from the past. How I am connected to those who have come and gone before me, what they have given me. I might love my versions of my own stories too much, they might become fixed if I don't take time to revisit.

The fourth step is practice. I assumed it was to learn a practice, to devote oneself to a prayer or a meditation practice, for example, a physical and spiritual practice, a learning practice. Or practice, like woodshedding in music, practicing your scales on the way to improvisation. That kind of practice.

But the Hebrew is *ma'aseh*, an elastic word that can mean story or account, a narrative, récit, a kind of collection of teachings around a subject, a shape to a certain subset of wisdom. Or in Yiddish, the more familiar *mayse*, a story, a version; to give the response, the wisdom, the teachings a shape, a context.

What follows is teaching. I assumed that by this time in the sequence, I might know enough to teach it. It might be a formal teaching, it might be by demonstrating what I have learned through what I do. It might be by my walk in the world, what I teach through how I live.

There is an alternate version in some manuscripts of this last principle. Instead of *moreh/morah* (teaching), there is a scribal difference *modeh/modah*, gratitude or thankfulness, an easy variation – the letter *dalet* for the letter *resh*. I have come to gratitude. Either/or or both, it works in every way.

In the year I am drawing this down, it is 1000 (1001) years since the birth of Ibn Gabirol. There have been many intersections that drew me to this project.

A thousand years in Your sight like a passing day, like a watch in the night (Psalm 90:4). He may not have written *Choice of Pearls* at all, but the pericope attributed to him stays with me as a guideline for spiritual practice:

Silence	שתיקה
Listening	שמיעה
Memory	זכרון
Practice	מעשה
Teaching	מורה
Thankful	מודה

Shtikah
Shemi'ah
Zikaron
Ma'aseh
Moreh, Morah
Some MSS. *Modeh, Modah*
Letter dalet or letter resh, common variation.

About the Source

Ibn Gabirol, from *Mivchar ha-Peninim*, Arabic original translated into Hebrew by Judah Ibn Tibbon, father of Samuel Ibn Tibbon, translator of Maimonides' *Guide to the Perplexed*. Quoted in an English version in 1859 under the title *A Choice of Pearls*, translated by B. H. Ascher.

Society for Hebrew Literature
Ascher, Benjamin Henry

Hebrew scholar and author; born in 1812 at Peisern (grand duchy of Posen); died Feb. 24, 1893, in London. His father, a corn-merchant, gave his son a careful religious and secular education. In 1840 Ascher went to England, where he soon mastered the English language, and, in 1843, was elected "ḳabranim rabbi" (funeral preacher) of the Great Synagogue. In 1847 he published a new edition of the well-known *Sefer Ḥayyim* (The Book of Life), with an English translation. In 1859 he published Solomon ben Gabirol's *Mivchar ha-Peninim* (A Choice of Pearls), embracing a collection of ethical aphorisms, maxims, and reflections, accompanied by an English text and explanatory notes. He wrote two other works of minor importance, *Initiation of Youth* (1850), a small catechism, and the ritual for the *Dedication of the House*. In 1884 he resigned his office, which he had held for over forty years. Ascher obtained from Sir George Grey several concessions for Jewish prisoners, to enable them to observe their religion.

Bibliography:

Jewish Chronicle, March 3, 1893, p. 8;
H. A. Löwy, Catalogue of Hebraica and Judaica in the Guildhall Library, pp. 93, 147, London, 1891.

From Jewish Encyclopedia, 1901.

Solomon Ibn Gabirol

Solomon ben Judah Ibn Gabirol (Shlomo ben Yehudah Ibn Gabirol), sometimes Gavirol on street signs in Hebrew. Arabic has no "v" sound and the -ol is a Spanish suffix, in Arabic he is Abu Ayyub Sulaiman Ibn Yahya Ibn Jubayrol (or Ibn Jabirul), later Avicebron, Avicembron, Avicenbrol, Avencebrol – a Latinized corruption of his name. I call him Ibn Gabirol, Spanish-Jewish poet of 11th c. Andalusia, often linked with poets Shmuel HaNagid, Moshe Ibn Ezra, Yehudah HaLevi. Moshe Ibn Ezra thought he was the best of them.

Borrowing from Arabic poetry and philosophy forms, mad at everybody, the poet Ibn Gabirol wrote out his revenge in verse both secular and spiritual. With the secular, he expressed his desires, his complaints, his vulnerabilities, his confidence, his regrets. With his spiritual poetry, he transcended.

Secular and spiritual, known and unknown, angry and elevated, Arabic forms, Hebrew references, Latin appropriations, Kabbalistic overtones, he was an in-between person. An outsider.

He also wrote philosophical poetry with a neo-Platonist lean. He has the distinction of being known under a corrupted name for a work in Latin much studied in Christian scholastic circles, *Fons Vitae*. He was known for that work under an Arabic corruption of his Hebrew name for eight centuries. Long after his lifetime, he was misunderstood.

His diwan (collection) almost lost, it was recovered from a pile of kindling scraps in Iraq by an antiquarian book collector. His secular work was literally plucked from the fire.

In the mid 19th century, about the same time that *Choice of Pearls* (the text from which I borrowed the structure for this piece) was translated into English, a blind Rabbi Salomon (Solomon) Munk fishing around the Bibliothèque Nationale in Paris demonstrated that the poet-philosopher thought to be a Christian or Muslim poet-philosopher responsible for the Latin *Fons Vitae* named Avicebron, was actually Ibn Gabirol.

His Hebrew version would have been entitled *Mekor Chayim* (the Arabic original has been lost), *Source* or *Fountain of Life*.

Ibn Gabirol, born in Malaga 1021-2, died in Valencia, by most accounts before the age of forty.

Name please.

Shlomo Ibn Gabirol
That's the son of Gabirol
Solomon
There, that's correct.

Occupation please –

Poet
Itinerant
Philosophe.

Preoccupations please –

Grammar I love grammar
And details
Eulogies a little death obsession
Philosophy in verse form
Singing
That kind of thing.

Location –

I was born in Malaga
About 1021-22 CE.

Known for –

Nothing.
Until a blind rabbi Salomon Munk

Rediscovered me in a library in Paris
Mid 19th century.

Sorry?

My name had become corrupted
I was known as Avicebron
Poet of Plato
They pored over me in the scholastic seminaries of Europe
Author of *Fons Vitae* (Latin)
That was me
Ibn Gabirol. Avicebron. Ridiculous I know.

Anything else –

I wrote *Adon Olam*
Master of the Universe
Part poetry part philosophy part spirituality
We call it a *piyyut* from the Greek for poet
I knocked out a thousand of them.

What else –

They were all jealous
I was the best of the poets
The legend: They killed me
Jealous poets
Buried me under a tree.

And –

And in years to come the tree bore
Uncommonly beautiful fruit
Revenge.

Anything else you want to be remembered for?

I yearned for a sweetheart
I wasn't so pretty
I would have been happier I suppose
But I wouldn't have been more
Productive.

Thank you.

When will this appear?
I want everyone to see it.

What I Want You To Do

Template for spiritual growth of Ibn Gabirol, from *Choice of Pearls*

Start with **Silence**.

Why start there?

Listen. That's the second step: **Listening**. Silence will open up the space for listening.

Oh. I get it, anticipating a flutter of language before it's cooked, so to speak —

Third, this one less intuitive, **memory**.

Remembering what?

Remembering what I know. I may have forgotten. What I've been taught. Who taught me. What has come to me from then, from them. Places in the heart I need to visit. Revisit. Calling up names. The names of my true self.

Oh, that's good.

Fourth, the deed. **A practice** I think it means. It could mean a **story**. An account. A version. But let's start with a practice.

A story. That's interesting, like an account, a set of teachings around a certain subject.

Could be. The word might mean an account or a story. A Version.

Version. As in give the teaching a shape. Shape it with words, infused with a remembering of sources, resources, teachings, inspirations, influences, a story rises out of what we know. Or a practice. A way to encounter challenges.

Or both. A version and a practice. Like a **spiritual practice**. Now the fifth: **Teaching**.

By embodying it or actually teaching it, more formally?

Both. By the way, there's a manuscript with a variation. Instead of teaching – **gratitude**. **Thankfulness**.

That's good. Either one is good.

Yes. Teach. Gratitude. **Teach gratitude**. Be it. Both are good. But note it's an alternate version. It's in the crawl space.

Shlomo's Back In Town

I used to visit a number of prisons. I felt that I was doing something important in the prisons, more than I realized when I started the project. I had three intersecting areas in my work-life that filled neglected spaces: In the prisons, in mental health/mental illness awareness and support, and in addictions. They were all difficult and all overlooked in my locality.

I felt an integrative sense that all avenues are connected and that the road through prison was not so isolated, separate, dis-integrated from the other roads of action and reaction, triumph and defeat, mistakes and repentance, curiosity and study. And every now and then I had an experience that brought the convergence home in a way I could not have made up.

One day I was visiting one of the prisons and after the teaching session there was alone time with a few of the prisoners. One of them, a particularly serious and well educated person, took me aside and asked if we could talk. Something private.

My mind went traveling in the few moments before he gave over what he wanted from me. I knew nothing about his background other than what I picked up in our lessons, I only knew what I had discerned from learning with him.

There were a few moments of awkward silence between us, more awkward I'm sure on my part. I figured this would not be a classroom type discussion. He spoke.

Who do you think wrote *Adon Olam*? He asked me. I stared at him for a long moment. Of all the subjects he might have brought up, this was the least expected. At that moment all my expectations came crashing into each other until they folded into the whole. My expectations were showing and the sense of the integrative truth of what we were living eclipsed the separate worlds – out there in here, up there down here, material spiritual, far away and right here, books and classrooms and prisons collapsed into one coherent whole.

I know more than a little about the *piyyut Adon Olam*. I have a special interest (obsession) about the setting where it may have arisen, I have studied the literary poetic aspects of the tone-poem as well as applied it to dozens of musical settings, a half a dozen I made up myself, and I taught the legend that it may have been a lullaby composed by one of my favorite poets Ibn Gabirol, 11th century. It's a subject I'm so deep into that I hesitate to share it unless I'm asked because it qualifies as an obsession and more interesting to me than almost anyone I encounter.

It's one of many secret preoccupations I try not to impose on others unless they are genuinely interested; this intersection of poetry, liturgy, music, spirituality, language, history, art, creativity. A person like me could be insufferable without a certain sensitivity with whom I am speaking. I practice restraint.

Adon Olam? I muttered, trying not to betray my surprise and delight, I have a few thoughts about that.

SILENCE

שתיקה

Silence

The Holy One was fiddling with the letters
when I returned.

"You will have a wonder teacher in the future.
What do you want with me?" I asked.

"Shush, find your silence," said the Holy One.

"Am I lost?" I asked.

"Nice-lost," said the Holy One, "good-lost. Lost enough you will
have to find your silence. Find your silence."

I went searching for my silence.

I came to the sea of tears. I sat with my memories until I recalled
every loss. I enjoyed each act of freedom as it was given and
taken away and everyone I have ever loved came to visit, one more time.

That's how I found my silence.

How Long

All of us could be humbler. We could live inside each other for
a while give up our certainty and earn the heart of
understanding.

We could say there is no other until we believed it.

We could take a G*d's** eye view, become small,
live within the skin of someone we do not understand.

We could all be quieter, sit within our heart – lines,
let the truth rise before us.

We could find our quiet, live in that quiet for a while.

We could all be kinder reserve judgment
delay certainty live with ambiguity.

What if we acted as if something fine is approaching and we
could be preparing waiting and quiet.

If we were quieter we might find our silence
we could step back from the edge and do nothing –

Until it became clear what to do what not to do.

As long as it takes.

** About the Asterisks
The asterisks within the name of G*d is a nod to the way I was taught.
Also a dash or a hyphen is flat but an asterisk sparks. And with every asterisk, a pause.

Everywhere

I see the workers in the upper and lower waters
gathering the streams into their arms.

Once the divine integration was made in my presence
delirious you said *I love the world.*

Did you mean all of it or some of it?

I track the ascents and descents
the upper root and the lower root will find each other
but don't leave me alone.

If the ends have been calculated
I have not seen them.

All my broken bones are whole
my broken heart too, every shard complete.

I love the partial the broken individual incomplete
the fragment the wounded the quiet.

I love the separate you said
because it integrates
and even if not
it is whole.

The Heart Feels

The heart feels a knocking
A spiritual knocking

A new and noble thought
Listening to the voice of an angel

An angel of G*d come knocking
On the doors of our soul

Make a small opening

Create something from what
The soul reveals

Gather up these sparks
Illuminate the world

Out of small truths

Big truth

—after Rav Kook

Bhante

He wore the orange robes of a Buddhist monk. He was from Cambodia, when he came to this country he settled in Stockton, California. I was told that he was 104 years old when I met him. I don't believe I had ever known anyone that old, but Bhante looked perhaps eighty years old. Honey skin, unwrinkled and soft, large hands for a small man, gentle fingers that did not tremble when he placed them on my daughter.

We went to the countryside to meet him, my wife, my son, one daughter, myself. He was staying with someone an hour from town. He was staying in a house in a subdivision in a rural area, not a likely place for a Buddhist healer I thought.

Inside the house was pleasant and we sat in a room with a floor to ceiling picture window of the trees surrounding the house. We sat in the room and watched the birds fly onto the porch outside the window and nibble from the bird feeders on the wooden balcony. My son was enchanted by the birds, and sat quietly on the couch watching the show outside the window, stringing beads for Bhante who was having soup for lunch in the next room. We were told he liked to have someone with him when he ate so our host was sitting with him at the kitchen table.

He took a long time eating. He went to the bathroom. He was wearing the orange robes I have seen Buddhists wear. Over the robe was a sweater vest with a breast pocket. In the breast pocket he had four pens, one Cross pen, and three other inexpensive pens, all different.

He was wearing on his wrist the beads that my son had just strung for him. He was small and the beads hung off his wrist onto his hand, the black beads set nice against his honey colored skin. A kind face, his head practically hairless his skin smooth. He was wearing the kind of bedroom slippers Grandpas wore, functional but not much for appearance.

He had set up homemade lights that he used in his healing. The lights were green, the kind that were used to grow plants. He had them all over the room and he turned them on and directed them toward my daughter.

Another woman arrived who lived in the area. We made small talk while Bhante was having soup. She had a radiation mark on her face, and when Bhante came out, her friend (our host) explained that she had a tumor on the back of her head and at the end of the month she would have it surgically removed. We sat together in a circle and Bhante began with my daughter.

He asked a few questions, spoke a few sentences, his English was good and not heavily accented.

He moved his chair to my daughter and positioned her so that the green lights were shining on her. He left his hand on her for a half an hour, forty five minutes. All of us closed our eyes, it was quiet and calm in the circle, my son was sitting on the couch watching the birds, my wife holding our little girl on her lap.

My son went out on the porch and watched the birds feeding in the bird feeder. The sun warmed the room through the picture window and some of us may have fallen asleep. Bhante sat still, moving his hand now and then to different places on my daughter.

My son came back into the room and sat on the couch. All of a sudden a baby blue bird came hurtling into the window. The bird hit the window hard and fell to the balcony. My son went out onto the balcony and he picked the bird up in his hands. It was small and it looked to me like its neck was broken but I didn't say anything. The bird was not moving.

My son took the bird in his hand and held it out on the balcony for about half an hour. He blew into his hand, he rubbed the bird just as he saw Bhante doing to his sister inside. We were watching from inside the living room, Bhante still focused on my daughter, my daughter having fallen asleep on my wife's lap, myself and our hostess sitting in the healing circle, the young woman from the neighborhood sitting with the back of her head to one of the green lights.

My son came into the house with the bird in his hands and showed it to Bhante. We all looked at the bird lying in his hands and again it looked to me like its neck was broken. It wasn't moving. Bhante looked up at him and said, "hold it in your hands, it will fly."

My son returned to the porch outside and continued stroking it, and after another twenty minutes the bird flew out of his hands and into the trees. Some of us had watched the whole drama from inside the living room. My son came back into the living room and sat on the couch. I went over and sat next to him. After a few minutes of sitting in silence together, he turned to me and said, "Dad, that was the greatest feeling of my life. I thought the bird was dead but its soul was still alive."

"Its soul was still alive," I repeated. And again, "its soul was still alive. Let's remember to tell each other this story every so often. Let's remind each other what we saw today."

I thought the Bhante story was finished. I wrote it and I let it sit. It was different from my other stories. This was one of the only stories I had written that I had not shown to anyone. It lacked the imagery and language of the other stories I was writing during the same period. I finished it and put it in a file in my story drawer where it remained undisturbed for five years.

During those years, I often thought about Bhante and the story. It's common that someone asks about one of my stories, did that really happen? I usually avoid answering because I feel that there is a quality about story that is true, whether it happened or not.

The Bhante story acquired a life of its own in a way different from my other stories. When I would think about Bhante and the events in the story, I asked myself the same question: Did it happen?

The story began to change in my mind. I wasn't sure that the events I wrote about had ever happened at all. When I read the story, it seemed like a tale found in the earth, written on a rock, a sound, not a story like the others. It didn't belong to me and so I didn't know what to say about its truthfulness.

I had not shared it with anyone. Then one day in July just before the turn of the millenium, I took the story nested deep in my files, the story called "Bhante," and sent it to a half a dozen of my friends. Some of them were friends I had never sent stories to before. It's as if it appeared by design on my screen.

I sent the story to M. I had never sent a story to M. A week after I sent him the story called "Bhante" he called me.

"Thanks for the story," M. said. "It was a beautiful eulogy to him."

"What do you mean?" I asked.

"That's why you sent it, isn't it, like a eulogy?"

"A eulogy?"

"Yes, a eulogy, on the occasion of his passing."

I asked him how he knew that Bhante had passed. I asked him if he knew anything else about Bhante. All I knew was his name and this tale.

"Sure, I know all about him. There was half a page on him in the New York Times," M. said, "the Sunday right around the time you sent the story. I assumed that's why you sent it . . ."

I hadn't seen the obituary and I knew nothing more of Bhante's existence than the name and the story that I had doubted had ever happened. I found the obituary in the Sunday edition of the New York Times, page 19, July 18, 1999:

Bellong Mahathera Is Dead;
Cambodian Monk was 110

The Venerable Dharmawara Mahathera, a high-ranking Buddhist monk who advised kings and prime ministers and established a new life after the age of 90 as a Buddhist leader in the United States, died on June 26 in Stockton, California, and his body was cremated as part of a 14-day ceremony that ended on July 10. He was 110.

The obituary explained that he was always called "Bhante, a Cambodian Buddhist honorific." M. had read that on the day he received and read my story.

Bhante had many students and disciples. He was an intimate of King Norndom Sihanouk of Cambodia, he was at the bedside of the first Prime Minister of India, Jawaharlal Nehru, when Nehru died.

At 90, Bhante moved to Stockton, California. "Ten years ago, when a gunman fatally shot five children and himself at a Stockton elementary school, Bhante showed up unsummoned within hours, conducting a ritual intended to dispel the gunman's ghost and to bring peace to the souls of the murdered children."

He was a judge in Cambodia before he became a monk. He married, had a child. He followed the Buddhist path, at one time going "into the jungle for six years to follow the ancient Thai Forest Tradition, eschewing shelter, meditating day and night at the foot of trees and eating only one light meal a day." His wife remarried. Every few years, he returned to Cambodia to see his daughter, who at the time of his passing lived in Seattle.

About the time that the 14-day ceremony after his death ended, Bhante's story that had sat in silence within me called and I sent it around.

Bhante's soul stirred in me to tell others that it had lived in the vessel of an old monk, that he had passed through our lives, our stories bound together in ways that clarified only as his soul paused and whispered to me, "remember me, tell the story as it happened."

add your notes here

LISTENING

שמיעה

Invocation

And all the people saw the voices and the torches the sound of the shofar and the smoking mountain and the people saw and trembled so they stood from afar.
—Exodus 20:15

Walk with me won't you please
help me over the floating
stairway underneath
my feet slip.

Without your everlasting arms
I might float away
another shore where someone else
will pick me up and bring me home.

Something known there in the blood
closer than breath the beginning of comfort
pull me to your chest your heart my heart
your science my science.

Be careful Compassion
assemble the healers
let us know if there is something
that cannot be revived.

Feeling for Pulse

The arc of language one finger on particulars
one finger on universals feeling for pulse
listening and opening beyond forms
beneath before and after language
in blood in bone.

Wild ride on the heart-line the seam
between past and future the present
challenging enough to require
full attention –

How we enter where we enter into the forest
to go deep and with seeds
planting.

O Holy Mother

O holy Mother if I were standing with you I wouldn't speak a word
I would sit in the dirt listening for silence.

I would leave the spigot onto tears open offer up my separation.

I would wear a big Bukharan hat on my head for humility
for respect I would wrap myself in fringes clutch the fringes
to my heart-line.

I would repeat the names of human beings a mantra of grief
for lives lost and lives found.

I would ask is G*d among us until I believed there was G*d within
or among or around until G*d was everywhere.

Then I would say to the persons sitting next to me right side
left side the names of my beloveds.

I would speak their names until I felt myself a fountain overflowing.

The fountain that I received from them would never go dry
I might become such a fountain myself some day.

Amen.

Sad and Beautiful

He picked up the horn. That's the unity, he said, he gave it
a good blast. The universal.

Then he blew again. That's the relative, he said, it's wavering,
a crying, a longing to return.

He blew again. Now we are breaking apart.

He blew once more. A greater blast. That's the promise of return,
he said.

It's a sad and beautiful world. Sad we drift away.
Beautiful we are hungry to return.

Your Inner Eden

Your inner Eden
Your pure side

Simple always
Uncorrupted by mind

There the G*dly light
Without boundary
Without restraint of intellect

Refined
This change of thinking

Receive from everyone
Your inner delight

Path of Blessing
Your inner Eden

—after Rav Kook

Vision

R. Gamaliel, R. Eliezer b. Azariah, R. Yehoshua, and R. Akiva
came to the Temple Mount
they saw a fox coming out of the Holy of Holies
they all burst into tears except Akiva.
Akiva laughed.
—BT, Makkot 24b

I saw the foxes on the narrow dirt roads of the lower Galilee inching my way along in a Spanish-built car and finding my way to my destination. I saw the foxes, it was the week before *Tisha B'Av* and there was nothing in the obvious associations lost on me. The foxes were small, car savvy, easily outrunning me on the car/foot/bike path darting in and out of openings in the foliage at the side of the road where they no doubt lived and thrived. Little foxes.

I felt neither the inclination to burst into tears nor to have a particularly optimistic read on the future, though the Akiva laugh is most meaningful to me as an invocation of neither via positiva or via negativa – via ambiguosa. Who knows what the foxes prefigure; you may as well laugh. The others thought it was desolate, Akiva thought it was funny. I think when presented with the sensory information one may as well laugh.

I also feel the proximity between laughing and tears, to me they are right next to each other on the circle of human responses to existence. Tears are sitting in one spot on the circle, right next to the tears is the funny man and the distinction between the two is subtle. You might think you're sitting in the tears spot and a moment later you realize you are in the next seat laughing. I spend a good deal of every day in both seats as do most of the people I love.

I recall the description of Bar Yochai the paradigm of mystical teachers,

Akiva's student: One eye smiling, one eye crying.

Akiva knew the prophecy from Zechariah 8:4ff: Old men and old women shall sit again in the streets of Jerusalem, each of the elders with staffs in their hands. The streets of the city shall be full of boys and girls playing in its streets.

So don't take this prefiguring of the foxes too seriously. Better days are coming. Akiva of the long look.

Or perhaps what Akiva had was a real vision. He actually saw into the future and witnessed what Zechariah described happening. It wasn't a matter of attitude or posture, it was Akiva gazing into the future and seeing so much restoration that the implication of the ruin brought by the foxes meant nothing to him. He might have been laughing at everybody else's limited imaginations. Akiva saw beyond that, he had confidence in the future and knew G*d provides. Relax, said Akiva, I saw it and quit making sermons. You're boring me with your tears drawn from those cute little foxes.

Secret: Every so often – what we have – is a real glimpse.

I was in Israel when I wrote this and the second or third evening after I arrived, I twisted my ankle in a rather dramatic way. I saw this at least a week before I came. I didn't tell anyone I saw it coming because I didn't believe it myself, it was just a dreamy imagining that I hurt my ankle when I came to the Land and I couldn't do much. I had myself a vision, I also didn't want my friends and family to think I'm crazy. It's just not comfortable.

There's a door that opens once in a while in my head and I look through or out. That's what I saw about two weeks before as I was preparing to leave the States: An injury, a foot or leg injury in Israel, myself laid up.

What I didn't see was the virus that followed, one I assume I picked up while visiting the Rambam Hospital in Haifa that really laid me out, drove up a fever that crashed the bell over my head and made me delirious for at least one night and achy and stomachy and prepared for a clean colonoscopy by day two of said Vee-roos [Heb.].

My handlers drove me to Jerusalem and dropped me in a hotel room by myself for a couple of days. But it was good. I felt like I was a street addict detoxing except I was overlooking the Old City, so much romance I could hardly stand it. Blake saw G*d outside his window when he was five. I don't doubt this at all. My own son picked out angels when he was just beginning to speak, his first word was "light." In the expressed environments of such spirits – not a trace. Build it and I will dwell within them, Exodus 25:8. Within them, not it. All the clues are in the holy Torah. We have to think like Sherlock.

As I wrote this, I was coming to my senses, having not left my hotel room overlooking the Old City of Jerusalem for several days. The hotel staff was kind, they knew something was wrong in my room but did not ask. I was in Israel to do some teaching, most of which I had to cancel out on, and to study with my music teacher with whom I had already sat enough to acquire my pieces which I diligently worked.

I had a load of books and the WiFi. I had a very tasty borrowed Turkish style oud and a lovely German guitar I purchased in Prague and kept in Israel because I had been studying there every summer with my musical muse. I made a pallet on the floor and didn't speak to anyone for days.

I didn't have that much to teach anyway. I had entered the listening curve of my life, having moved through the talking curve as a young man when I had the hubris to think I knew something. I am on the less is more track, find your silence, listen, give it all away track.

Because of the injury I spent much of my time laid out on the floor in a hotel overlooking the Old City of Jerusalem. I played lying on the floor, often sleeping in fever with the borrowed oud at my side.

I shared my obsessions and inspirations with my old friend Zach. I have known Zach since he was a little boy. Zach had grown up and acquired the oud obsession, much exceeding my ability on the instrument. Now we had become collaborators. I had written to Zach and told him about the vow I had taken to write a piece for every portion of the Torah based on the text and inspired by the *maqam*, the musical form, for that portion.

From Jerusalem I wrote to Zach and this time he responded with: Why don't we put the pieces you wrote and the *maqams* together? Let's record them. Let's create a new form.

I wrote this in my journal that summer from the floor of the hotel: *I have entered into an adventurous challenge project today, presented it to my collaborator and am delighted to begin not knowing at all where it will lead. If anywhere.*

By this time Zach had deepened himself in the Syrian-Jewish tradition of *maqam*. The *maqam* is a musical structure underneath eastern Mediterranean Jewish and Arabic music. Zach worked with a synagogue community in New York who sponsored a year of videos featuring one of my pieces and music Zach put together to correspond to each weekly Torah reading.

We recorded the pieces live all over New York City with a professional group of musicians he convened.

We called it "The Maqam Project." In its first incarnation, we recorded a piece for every portion of the entire Torah. *What were you doing in New York?* I was asked the several years it took to complete the project.

Recording the Torah.

Zach and I then worked the audio on the pieces that were dearest to us and we created a double CD: *L'Oud and the Abstract Truth.*

Afterword

I passed away in Jerusalem. It was some kind of strange Kawangee fever that I picked up over the African Asian rift where germs wander when they are bent on revenge.

Until my death, I never once subscribed to the germ theory.

When found I was laid out on a pallet on the floor of a hotel room cradling a tasty Turkish oud in my arms with a look of such ecstasy on my face that the room keepers thought I was sleeping for two days. Then they decided I was dead.

They wrapped me in a sheet and went about looking for who I was. I left few clues.

They held my funeral between two groves of olive trees. The officiant was a blind holy man, perhaps a woman ("there are so many more than two possibilities," s/he said when asked), who was called Tiresias, an irony in the Land but just right for the essential ambiguity of the way I experienced existence in the sacred and ridiculous.

Tiresias described me as light and sound; my soul a luminescent blue, my sound the hum of insects at night.

Of course I wasn't dead. I revived. I only seemed to be dead.
I returned home and went to work.

MEMORY
זכרון

The Prince and The Rooster

From Rebbe Nachman, 1772 – 1810,
the Chassidic story master

I ran into Jimmy in Detroit. He told me that not too
long ago he had lost his mind thought he was a rooster.

Where was this?

California. I took off all my clothes, Jimmy said, lived
under a table wouldn't eat anything but grain and
chicken food.

Then Prince the guitar player came took off all his
clothes got under the table began to act like a rooster too.

We swore friendship to each other and slowly slowly
Prince began the healing.

He put on a shirt, I put on a shirt. I said to Prince, do you
really want to dress like a human being? You know what
Prince said to me?

I think so, but tell me anyway.

Prince said just because you dress like a human being
doesn't mean you have to cease being a rooster.

The next day we ate at the lunch counter in the bowling
alley. Prince ordered a tuna sandwich.

You gonna eat like a person too? I asked Prince.

You can eat like a human being and still be a rooster. You

can do anything and still be the rooster you are.

That's how it worked for me, Jimmy said, Prince saved me slowly slowly.

He taught me I can do anything and remain the rooster I am.

Blessings We Call Whole

In silence he began alone
Before the incantation of sources
He went to the well himself
Placed a mark on his forehead
Practiced remembering this way
Memory of deepest self
Returning
With the help of a holy fellowship of similarly gifted souls
Drawn to the same sources
They could not have been more different in all other ways
When they ended their days of preparation
They gave away what they had been given

This they called teaching

The Eulogizers

He wore his soul like a coat
inside out
snatched a hundred others away from the precipice
because he had been there.

He had turned the beast
left a wife and kid
dropped over at the gym.

The eulogizers arrived
with their scripts and suits.

Their words had no lift.

Say something.

Say nothing said Buffalo
descend into the dark
go alone without a flashlight
sit silently on the floor
be cold
let your bones freeze
without heat without light.

Resist the temptation to speak.

Make no jokes
wait for the story to rise.

How long?
As long as it takes.

In the world of truth Buffalo said
you get what you deserve
what didn't happen in the upside-down world
in the world of truth the tale is told differently
you get what you want
in the world of truth, said Buffalo.

Here in the upside-down world
you have to stand on your head to make sense.

Janine's Terrible Inheritance

Janine buried her father today
After changing his past
She overflowed like a fountain
And gave birth again to her children
She spilled into her own past as well

"How so?" She asked, to no one in particular
But I was near and I had been thinking about the old rabbis
And their holy companions who turned it and turned it
Settled on the mystery algebra of generations –

How the right action of the present can transform the past
Nudge, budge, move G*d's holy arm
When you thought it could not be moved
And I realized I might love G*d more
With less certainty

Almost A Great Funeral

On the sacred balance sheet
something had to be corrected
a repair in the cosmic loam
an indignity done
in the realm of memory, spirit,
where G*d and soul
the mystery quantities calculate
in a Zoroastrian tug for the heart of the world
as if the world turns on these corrections
which it does
spins right around on the axis of Jackie.

We buried Jackie last week.

At one point I felt loaded into the catapult
and hurled into the sky where I exploded
into a thousand sparks
light into light
drifting back to ground like Chinese fireworks.

There are so few of these moments nowadays.

When Jackie passed
I thought she could have saved the world
her ruthlessness saving souls
she went to the edge with people
because she had been there herself
snatched them back as she had been
as if she made the necessary repairs
as if she were the true person of compassion
we have been waiting for every night to renew the next day
then the question —

what if there are not enough of them
what then?

How many true persons of compassion does it take?

For a few minutes remembering Jackie
I felt the possibility of redemption
that's when I took off
shot up into the overhead air
and dissipated into the wind around her grave.

If the priestliness had spent five minutes
listening to her story
he could have taken the whole crowd there
gone with us anyway.

If he had understood
how Jackie transformed and redeemed herself
and dozens of others
we could have explained to him
that Jackie might have cleaned up all the mess
through the first person she snatched back
for to save one person is to save an entire world.

What a shame to have missed the whole story
when even a part of it
one person
one of many that Jackie saved
could have redeemed
all of us.

Ben-Zion's Grave
or A Great Artist Is Buried in Israel

When he died, Ben-Zion left instructions to be buried in Israel, in a cemetery not far from the sea in Haifa.

My friend Todd chronicled the work of Ben-Zion in photography during the last ten years or so of Ben-Zion's life. Ben-Zion died in 1987. Todd led me to the work of Ben-Zion, to his life and his art. It all felt familiar to me, though I had never seen any of it before, nor had I heard of the artist. I felt as if I had been taken by the hand and drawn into his circle.

> A light sound
> like the thinnest of threads
> accompanies me in the darkness of the abyss.
> God forbid
> if this thread should break
> I am like one lost in the endlessness.
> This sound from the beginning of
>   my childhood
> like a voice in the endlessness
>   of life
> accompanies me wherever I turn.

Ben-Zion was also a poet. He was born in 1897 and started out as a poet writing in Hebrew but after his emigration as a young man to the United States he realized there was no audience for a poet writing in Hebrew in New York City.

Sometime around the rise of the Nazi brutality, Ben-Zion transformed into a visual artist as if he ascended into silence and memory. *Where's your poetry?* He was asked by a poet friend many years later. *Under my bed.*

He never stopped writing poetry, and I found several books of his poetry with drawings published in Israel by a small publishing house in Tel Aviv. He translated his poetry into English himself.

Ben-Zion would have been one hundred years old in the year I came to know of him, 1997. He was born Ben-Tzion Weinman in what is today western Ukraine, the son of a cantor who taught him Hebrew. His father was a third generation cantor and a composer of liturgical music, and his mother a storyteller.

He cultivated the literary language Hebrew, creating a poetry in Hebrew as did Bialik and others in the early twentieth century. They were creating a house without a home, a language without a place. Ben-Zion was passionate for Hebrew as a young boy, playing with words as he played with the stones that he collected his entire life.

Ben-Zion gathered pebbles, old iron tools, implements, and driftwood. He dragged home the natural shapes and materials and created art with them.

When he was 16, he took a room at the outskirts of his town, the same town Chagall came from, supporting himself by giving Hebrew lessons. When asked who his teachers were, whether it was possible at all to learn art from a teacher, he said, *yes, go into the woods. Pick up a stone. Look at it. Turn it over. Look at it.*

Ben-Zion's father died in 1920, and Ben-Zion and his mother came to the United States. Ben-Zion came to America with a knapsack filled with Hebrew plays and poems and his father's musical manuscripts and little else. They settled in New York City and that's where Ben-Zion stayed. He dropped his last name Weinman.

One name is enough for an artist, he said.

In the Thirties, Ben-Zion became a member of a circle of artists who called themselves The Ten. The tenth was expected but never appeared. The Ten included Mark Rothko and Adolph Gottlieb, Ilya Bolotowsky, Louis Schanker, John Graham, Earl Kerkam, Bob Godsoe, and Joseph Solman. They exhibited together until 1942. Alone among the ten (nine), Ben-Zion stayed with traditional religious ideas and images.

His work reflects all his interests, obsessions, and inspirations: The arts of antiquity, the images and characters of the Hebrew Bible, and language. He never stopped composing poetry in Hebrew and though he published only a small amount of poetry, the Hebrew letters and vowels also preoccupy Ben-Zion's visual work; the form, the shapes of Hebrew letters, words, diacritical points transformed into isolated icons of language and art through painting, sculpture, and a variety of other media.

His paintings reflect his vision of the dream-myth of the Jewish people, our heroes depicted with large, accepting hands, King David cuddling his harp, big feet on all of them, hands hiding the face of a woman lighting the candles, and his poetry.

My friend Todd, Ben-Zion's photographer-chronicler, came to Israel on a mission from Ben-Zion's wife Lillian to find her husband's grave. Ben-Zion had been buried in Israel. Lillian instructed Todd to place some of Ben-Zion's stones on his grave site, take pictures, pay respects, and to draw me into the circle. I was living in Jerusalem at the time.

Todd and I took to the road in my car and drove north. Todd had an address that turned out to be the burial society in Haifa. We found the office in the central city of Haifa, a small bureaucratic nightmare of an office, at just about the time when all of Jewish Israel releases its great exhalation before Shabbat.

The men with black hats and fringes in the office weren't interested in our request to look up a grave site until I mentioned, in Hebrew, that my friend Todd was a devoted student of a great master who is buried there. *His student has come to honor his teacher*, I told the burial society men, *by visiting his grave and leaving stones and saying prayers.* The men in the office dropped what they were doing, booted up the computers, found Ben-Zion on the list and offered to take us to the cemetery. We settled for a hand-drawn map. We had passed by the cemetery on our way into Haifa.

Todd and I found the cemetery on a hill not far from the Sea just south of town. We found first a large military cemetery, a great sprawl of a cemetery just off the road as one approaches Haifa from the south. This was the place to which we had been directed. There were soldiers walking in the cemetery; it looked as if there had been a large military funeral that day. Everyone was hurrying home, it was even later into the great exhalation than our visit to the burial society office. Here there seemed to be no one at work or in charge.

I saw a man who looked like a caretaker, it was Friday afternoon and he was rushing to leave. I asked him to help us find the grave. He didn't understand at first my formal Hebrew so I simplified the language. He, too, was going home. He couldn't help us. Then I told him the same thing I told the men in the burial society office, I introduced Todd as a student of the great artist Ben-Tzion Weinman who is buried somewhere in this cemetery. *He has come to give honor to his teacher.* The caretaker asked me if I had a car, he told me to retrieve it and meet him at the entrance to the cemetery.

I got the car and drove to the entrance and there he was waiting for us, he jumped into the back seat, took us up the hill to another cemetery and guided us through the grave sites to Ben-Zion's grave.

We found Ben-Zion's grave just as the sun began to make its way home in the West. I asked the caretaker to help us. The sun was hot that day, he was wearing one of those faded hats that resemble a sailor's hat with the flaps down. *For a hundred shekels I'll take care of its repair*, he used the word *tikkun* which has a simple and a sophisticated sense. We gave him some cash.

On the gravestone was written Ben-Zion's name, including his last name Weinman, also a quotation from one of his poems in Hebrew and the dates of his birth and his death in the traditional Jewish manner in Hebrew letters, corresponding to 1897 and 1987.

Todd and I stood at the grave and cleaned it off, Todd placed some stones on the head stone, took pictures for Lillian back in New York. On Ben-Zion's grave are the following words, in Hebrew only, from one of his poems:

Alah shiri vo kha-sha-char	עלה שירי בו כשחר
Hei-ir bi et olami	העיר בי את עולמי

My song rose up in me like the morning star
Awoke in me my world (trans. Ben-Zion)

We left the rocks on Ben-Zion's grave, Todd took pictures, we stood in the hot sun and read the poem written on the monument. The caretaker with the sailor's hat asked us, *are you family?* No, I reminded him, I said in Hebrew *he is a famous artist from America and we are his students. Ah, good, good*, he said, under the hot Levantine sun here where gravediggers approved of the notion that students were forever connected to their teachers, that all teachers and students were bound up together like souls over the great divide.

When I returned to the States, I became close with Lillian Ben-Zion and visited with her often. She was a guide for me, one of the few who could tell me: This is your work. This is not your work.

PRACTICING

מעשה

Exercises in Uncertainty
that Resolve in Embrace

Try sitting by yourself in a hospital waiting –
within they are working on someone you love
you are alone looking out a window, now throw up your arms
let yourself be taken up by the hands of a G*d
look out over the mist of your city
see the dome in the distance, let your vision
drift up to the sky set with clouds, dark, light.

Let your G*d expand just then.

Hold on tighter, let your large G*d
lift you. Ascend, look down, send a message
from your perch in the sky, draw it like a billboard
with a ribbon of light set against the threatening clouds.

Blow the clouds away
if you can.

All The Goods

Master of all the Goods
Scattered as they are

The physical is demanding to be fixed first
A physical practice

We are full of blemishes
Skirmishes and wars

The treasure of life –
Whose vision of existence yours?

Establish a world
And give it stature

The failings all necessary
Even when immersed in light

Shades and darkness
All around

I am not afraid
Lean in

—after Rav Kook

Don't Say Goodnight

You want to say something correct
Something so wise
In case you don't get another opportunity
Maybe you should hug her
Tell her that you had been brought into the world
Just for this moment
To comfort her
You were there at her birth
You stood by her bedside in the hospital
You sat with doctors in the fluorescent rooms
With diagrams of her insides on the wall
Just for this moment
You held her mother in the hallway
Before every surgery
You walked back and forth in the waiting rooms
You sat by the bed while she healed
You took her to the park in a wheel chair
You played catch with her on the lawn
To arrive just at this time
Say the right thing
You walked her to school
You prayed for her to grow up
Visit you in your old age with her beloved
You might tell her
Right now
This moment
When she needed to hear it
The one or two sentences
That will calm her
You want to tell her that you will not sleep
Until she gives you the privilege
Of speaking the right words

You want to tell her this
But you want first to absorb her hurt
Your face on her face and inhale it like breath
So she will sleep
Even when you
Cannot.

A Prayer for Her Healing

All the accompanying angels appeared for her because it takes a squad
a platoon of angels a division
Moroccan prayer beads pinned to the surgery bed
and the General
to make a complete healing.

Later in the night when everyone sleeps
they parachute in from the east and west
angels ascending descending
they wander in from the coasts.

Some have satchels slung over their shoulders filled with amulets
others with gifts.

All the energies converge for her
who lies silent in the dark with her mantra.

Her mantra.

It was not:
help me help me help me save me
amen.

But it could have been.

Or it could have been another prayer for healing
a specially created voice howling in the square
the words suspended between thought and deed
not wishes but why not
why not a wish
with her hands clutched to her chest
right hand buried in the left.

Why not a wish or a prayer or a whisper
she sneaks away for a chat with G*d.

Come on G*d get inside this
just this once
and G*d said
hold on

I'm coming.

The Failure of All Else

You know what it feels like
sitting on your hands to keep from floating away

you know what it's like
to hang from the edge with your fingertips

pay no attention to the pundits
and other sources of common wisdom

save yourself
sing

My Teacher

First meeting.

I stood in the corner of the dean's office when a shortish man, sandy hair, long eyebrows rakishly twirled, rushed in reading in Yiddish a letter he had received that morning from Israel. Slavic accent. He was wearing a monocle over his right eye and pressed his face into the paper.

"It's about Rivka, she was so beautiful, everybody was dying for her. She would kiss nobody! She was poison. She let nobody near her except Mottl. He kissed her in the big drawer under the hardware table –"

"In the drawer?"

A student had walked into the office at that moment carrying the mail.

"A big drawer underneath the hardware table where Itzik kept his aprons and coat, they climbed in and fell asleep, Itzik came in and pulled the drawer open and there they were, they ran away like doggies."

"Who . . . " the student said.

I was standing in the corner, the dean was smiling and he introduced me to my new teacher.

Later my future teacher grabbed me in the cafeteria line and we sat together while he shoveled great mounds of food into his mouth and sprayed me with sauce. He made puns on my name in three languages.

"I like you, come to the College, be my student."

He grabbed my hands and looked at my fingers, "you will have to start again, the texts the tunes they will speak to you. But you will start fresh. I will help you."

Later, I was telling John the tuba player about him and what it was like to be his student. "That's the way it is with music," John said, "someone has it, you want it, you learn how to get it. Anything can happen, sometimes wonderful, sometimes terrible. All mixed up together. That's the way you learn from a master."

I told John the rabbinical story about the student hiding under the master's bed.

"What did you learn?" the student is asked.

"I watched him put on his shoes."

"That's the way it was with my teacher," said John, "he taught us basics, like don't make excuses, practice, be prepared, trust G*d. We learned the fundamentals: How to shine your shoes, how to tie your tie. He was merciless about details. I worshipped the man, but there were many who didn't."

"Yeah, same here."

I told John how I had given away too much of myself to my teacher sometimes.

After I left him, my teacher came to see me work. He arrived early, sat in the pew (we were renting from a Church) and picked up a songbook stuck in the seat in front of him. About halfway through the service, he put down the book and closed his eyes. Afterwards he hugged me, then told me something that was as insightful as anybody has ever said about what I was reaching for through my work.

It was my mission, now given words, by my teacher.

A few days later he sent me a letter with a full critique, from the color of the seats to the look of the building from the road ("like a giant phallus held up by a square testicle on the ground").

He closed with, "I knew that I had just witnessed the opening of a human flower."

This is how it began. He handed me a guitar without strings, instructed me to play. "Like this," he said smiling, a mouth full of food, wiggling his fingers.

add your notes here

TEACHING

מורה

Tutorial

Will you be my teacher?
I asked him.
Certainly.
How?
Like this, and he threw himself off a cliff.
I went up to the heights
and looked below.
Above me sky
below the sea, the rocks.
Go, I heard.
Later I bled all over my back pack.
My teacher exploded into a thousand sparks.

And also like this, he said.

Please

Surprise me, lift me off to somewhere new
send me on a roundabout way
but make it a common journey
one that I know I would have taken
if not for this if not for that.

Too far out of my perimeter
I might not go with you.

Use your own words the idiosyncratic ones
the ones that tumble in your head
when you speak them in the wrong crowd
they look at you slant.

Don't tell me too much.

Smuggle in an organizing notion
sneak it past the guardians of equanimity
then ease past the conversationalists
the ones who speak loftier than I do.

They snatch away the lowly the uninspired
their standard is high language and gesture
only those great tortured Southern drunks in heaven
aspire to and the circle of intellectuals from Detroit
who sit in my mind and discourse
always alert to the cliché the untoward
the inelegant the symbolically over-fleshed.

They guard my perimeter like coyotes on the hunt.

My teachers the owl-eyed Reines
in his work shirt and heavy boots
and the others sit in faculty Senate.

Dr. Lehman who speaks slowly
draws on five civilizations he quotes from memory.

Dr. Fish roaming through the texts of a dozen
ancient libraries on three continents
they are inside me and a tough gang to penetrate.

Be thoughtful and push your ideas
the best you can through them won't you.

They are merciless on language.

Be a thinker a word maven
sweet singer of the unconventional soul
and please remember Mihaly chewing on his pipe
will be standing in the final circle of review
he will be saying this -- something
I might have put in his mouth
or he said it:

I need meaning.

It completes me.

Shape and Sense

A popsicle within the obscuring smoke
of his last ciggie
the old rooster
flat on his bed
the Cambridge tongue intact
though he had broke out of Glasgow
to speak that way.

He would live for another month.

On the bed crossword puzzles
his sister had sent from the London papers.

"A clue in context
another clue in form" –
this the last teaching from the overflowing fountain.

He shaped with words the shifting content
caught the ideas mid-thought
lassoed them with rope
rode them with wings and stirrups
above the fray.

Everything he said
appeared in the air above his head.

We carried him on a four postered platform
a palanquin around the city
trailing his ribbon of words
and everywhere we went
the people bowed
held out their hands
in spontaneous gestures of quiet gratitude

As if to thank him for being the soul of the generation
because it was clear
that he was the one we had been waiting for
to remind us who we are –
what we are all about.

My Soul Fell Out My Nostrils

My soul fell out my nostrils and broke onto the floor. I had used that image earlier that evening. Talia, six years old, the daughter of my acquaintance, was present at that session Friday night shul. Later as we were walking from the car into the Rabbi's house I couldn't put off her inquisitive little kid mind who seized on an image I had spoken earlier during the singing.

How did your *neshamah* (soul) fall out your nostrils and break onto the floor? I was trying to understand her question against what she had learned or she knew about the nature of the soul, the *nefesh* or the *neshamah*, that she might have imagined in a particular way, the way she had learned it. I had told a story about the *neshamah*, an additional soul, inside the tune *Yom Zeh L'Yisrael*.

I don't remember a darn thing any adult said that weekend.

To an adult, I would have said, or would have wanted to say, it's an image, a metaphor, I said it/wrote it the best way I could. The interpretation is yours. But I looked at her and asked, how old are you?

Six years old.

Six years old, her head working my image, my head turning the question not to dismiss her with a bent reed as it is written, this is a thoughtful kid. I turned her question over trying to find the words that could give it to her the way she was asking.

I could have patted her on the head, I suppose, what a smart question, cute kid, but I was dignifying the question from this six year old kid this no ordinary kid, and she probably hears in one form or another what a cute kid good question thank you honey, etc., plenty but not a real answer to her heavy toting mind.

I was almost frozen in my tracks by this kid. She was seeing that image I planted in her mind and maybe I could give her something by way of embellishment, maybe she was asking for some clarity, violating all my rules for writing something carefully and telling readers/listeners what it means.

I felt I should give her something that was at least as sincere as weighty as the challenge my word-picture had occasioned in her mind. Remembering she was six years old and I was not that practiced explaining poetry, or entering into deep dialogue with six-year-olds though I have reared two six-year-old girls of my own but it had been a while.

It took me some stumbling in my own language and thought (the time from the exit from the car to cross the street and enter the front door of the house) to find the appropriate response.

Do you remember what I said after my *neshamah* fell from my nostrils and broke on the floor? I asked. I followed it home and I've been following it home ever since. It's leading me back home because sometimes you can lose your *neshamah*, that's the point of the story of it falling out my nose, it's *as if* it fell out my nostrils, *it's like* it fell out my face and broke onto the floor because it's delicate, this *neshamah*, this quality we call soul. It can be lost and it can be broken.

And it can be found.

That was the point of the story I was telling: I was refiguring the notion of the additional soul into the idea of an inner life strength-source that can get lost even broken and that fragile, breakable, source inner power strength can be squandered or can be gathered up again and it can lead a person home, and for me I had been in that place once or twice when I had lost that soul power and when I am singing or talking about the additional soul, I am talking about following it home. Lost and found.

I said something like this to six-year-old Talia and in the jazz of responding to her question I realized I explained it pretty well. It was now clearer to me than it was before because Talia asked the question and I turned myself inside out to respond to it. I was done. I articulated an idea I didn't have before, a fresh entry into that image because this six-year-old kid asked a good question.

This was the authenticating conversation of the weekend for me, among other events not all so happy and simple, then something even more wonderful happened:

I looked at her and asked, do you understand that?

I know I had gone lofty and that face looking up at me with her question about the *nefesh* or *neshamah* falling out the nostrils both of us paused in front of the door about to enter the house where we would mark the end of that chapter of the encounter.

Do you understand what I'm talking about? Does that make sense to you?

She looked up at me and out into the space above her head and said something that topped off the conversation at its peak:

I think so.

She could have said yes and we would have been polite and done. She could have said no and probably ended any continuation of dialogue.

But she said full with the continuing struggle of human beings to come to grips with ideas in motion, in her vision six years old, in the universal struggle to make sense that she will no doubt be preoccupied with for the rest of her life –

I think so.

I loved that more than anything yet spoken, the sense of struggle with ideas and the hint I heard in her precocious soulful six year old intelligence that my mind my soul my heart is busy working these ideas and pictures that you have planted in me and now she has bounced them back. We were both growing through the encounter.

She came to the gig the next night, the only kid who did. She made her Daddy take her. She fell out early but not before we sat together on my box drum. I held her hands and her Daddy snapped a picture of Talia and myself grinning our conspiratorial smile of coaxed wisdom, something we shared on a weekend on the desert, when I was visiting and Talia preparing to move with her family to their next adventure.

I wrote the story on the airplane as I winged my way home on Sunday, dedicated it to my friend Talia and her parents, who will no doubt have a few conversations with their daughter about its contents.

I wrote it no differently than I would have written it for adults, though I wrote it for a six year old kid and I thought about that but someone once might have written a story for me, it may have been a reach for me to get what it was this story, but I followed it up, it led me into words and ideas that I would grow into knowing there was something there to aspire to, to grow into, something to reach for, so I left it in my language and maybe her parents will read it to her in the future and talk it out, who knows — I let it loose.

All stories, all poems, all songs, they belong there leading us or waiting for us watching over us teaching us and when it's time, we meet.

THANKFUL
מודה

Blessing

I will bless you and increase you as the earth
as the sands of the seashore as the sea
look at the algae now
and the horseflies buzzing around your face
I will make you as great as the algae as the grasshoppers.

Look up now to the sky you will be as great as the stars
as the darkness too you will be as great as the darkness
as the sand and the sea and the stars
the mud and the dark and the green
the sticky stuff on the surf
the early rains and the later rains
the mud the mud the green the sand the dark.

You will be a blessing
as great as the dark
the sea
the sand
the green
the flies.

Three Steps

Every day I get up and present
I take three small steps and place myself

What's my assignment

Make me a vessel

I am I say
I am you say
Let us be *I am* for each other

Your moves inspire me

Because you've gotten up every morning and said
Master of the Universe
Into Your hands I entrust my spirit

With my spirit
My body too

G*d is with me

I shall not fear

Narrow Bridge

We were sitting out in front of the coffee shop, myself and my teacher.

Teacher: How afraid are you? Before you answer, listen to me. Don't make yourself crazy.

Me: That's not a great thing to tell a kid who might be sitting alone with dark thoughts. Or a depressed adult.

T: You might get depressed. I've been depressed. There's always reason to be depressed and then there's depression without reason.

Me: I think there is a sadness associated with existence.

T: Of course. You might come to a gate or a bridge and the gate will be closed or closing or hard to push through, the bridge is narrow. But you move ahead.

Me: Then what?

T: You might have to pass over a narrow bridge. And the principle is not to make yourself afraid.

Me: Don't be afraid?

T: I didn't say that. There are reasons for fear. Don't add to them. Don't make yourself afraid. I heard there is a tree in Ukraine whose leaves take 100 years to grow. Time takes time. Patience.

Me: Patience.

T: Find some good inside, within yourself. Attach to it. Strengthen yourself with whatever you can find within, no matter how small and glue yourself to it. Find your strength. Be thankful for it. What's that you're doing?

Me: Writing.

Harmonizing Voice

Harmonizing voice among all voices
The one that unifies
Lifts and straightens out

From the fullness of worlds
To every creature

We are inner beings
Kidneys and kishkes

Mixed up in noise
Exalted thought

Songs to free the precious soul
Prepare to receive

Pouring oil in the
Oasis of wisdom

—After Rav Kook

At the Edge of the World

At the edge of the world there is a mountain, on this mountain there is a rock and from this rock springs the purest water in the world. At another edge of the world beats the Great Heart of the World, which gazes all day at the mountain. The Great Heart, filled with love, yearns for the water but it cannot have it. One move and the Great Heart would lose sight of the mountain and in that instant the world would die. But every evening when the sun goes down, the Great Heart sings to the Spring. And all hearts at the same moment sing to each other.

There is a true person of compassion who gathers up these fragments of song and pulls them together into Time. Just enough for another day.

A fragment from a fragment, a story told by Rebbe Nachman the story master, I brought down the story from the fragment that S. Ansky lifted from R. Nachman and included in Ansky's play *Der Dybbuk*. The story in another form is found in "Seven Beggars," one of R. Nachman's classic stories.

In the version of the Nachman story I know, yearning was a condition of existence. The emphasis was not on the object of yearning, but on the condition of yearning. Waiting.

The story is given as a wedding present. At the end of the story, the world is sustained by love. And longing. And poetry, song, and verse. The Great Heart of the world gives Time as a gift, a day at a time.

In the story there is a true person of compassion, without that person the fragments of song, the longing, would have no resolution. Like the story in the Talmud brought down from Abbaye, waiting is essential to all these stories.

Abbaye said, "there are not less than 36 *tzaddikim*/righteous persons in the world who receive the *Shekhinah*/the Divine Presence," from the Babylonian Talmud, Sanhedrin 97b, Sukkot 45b. Because they are waiting for _____, for whomever, they are waiting.

It was the waiting in the story that drew me in, like the yearning in the fragment of the Nachman tale.

What follows Abbaye's teaching in the Babylonian Talmud is the discussion between Rav and Shmuel, as if to imply: What if there is not enough righteousness? I often feel like I'm living inside that conversation, like I went for a swim in the sea of Talmud and bumped into someone I know.

Rav said, "all the ends have passed, and the matter . . . depends only on *teshuvah*-transformation and good deeds."

Shmuel says, "it is enough for the mourner to stand in mourning."

By Rav, everyone will have to transform, a great *teshuvah*, but by Shmuel, it is enough to stand in our suffering, to be with our mourning.

In Abbaye's teaching, every generation requires thirty-six righteous persons who receive G*d's presence. It's a minimum, they authenticate the generation. They are known as *lamed-vov-niks* (legendary "thirty-sixers").

Rav: I am thinking about Abbaye's teaching, that there are not less than thirty-six in the world who receive the Divine Presence.

Shmuel: Yes. Continue.

Rav: What if there came a generation in which there were less than thirty-six righteous individuals? A place or a generation. It could happen. Like Sodom. Like the generation of Noah. Like Auschwitz. Not enough righteousness.

Shmuel: What then? How would the world be redeemed?

Rav: A complete transformation, everyone would have to transform.

Shmuel: There would be only one thing to do: To stand in our suffering, a person at a time. To be with our sadness, the deep sadness of a world or a place in which thirty-six did not exist. In a sense to weep ourselves well.

Something else. All three of them, Abbaye, Rav, Shmuel, were *rashei yeshivah*, heads of academies, the three major academies of the Babylonian diaspora during the time the Babylonian Talmud was being collected.

Rav: The world will require a complete transformation, every one of us, or a complete social redemption, don't you think?

Shmuel: Even if there is a great catastrophe, or when there is such a catastrophe, perhaps we will sit in our sadness, we will be waiting for the inevitable redemption. Just as the catastrophe may be inevitable – so is the redemption. This I feel in my blood, in my bones.

Rav: Poetic.

Shmuel: Yes. I can be grateful. And unafraid. When I'm done crying I'm getting up and on with it. New world.

I met an American painter in Italy. Occasionally the painter told us a story that was tender, sometimes salacious. Of the latter stories, he said "all these stories end up with my clothes off." In all the stories there was a softness, sometimes even weeping when he told them.

One night he told us a story about himself and his Italian girlfriend looking for a village in the mountains near Assisi. I wasn't sure which category of story we were in – would the story erupt into holiness or end with his clothes off? Or both.

They came upon an old man walking with a stick. "An old peasant man," the painter described him. "We asked him where Assisi was. 'Oh. . .' he said, 'you mean città di San Francesco,' the city of St. Francis – that's how he knew it – how beautiful is that, the city of San Francesco. Francis lived in the eleventh century! We wept for a while and continued on our way."

It was the weeping that attracted me to his story, also to Shmuel's argument from the Talmud, weeping the world well, and a loyalty to Source-material; the old peasant man knew the town as the città di San Francesco.

The redemption is elusive, like Rav we will have to transform – one person at a time – and get on with the work of repair.

We are waiting. An active waiting. Sitting with Shmuel in our sadness, preparing for a new world.

In the Nachman story there is redemption from the true person(s) of compassion, one person at a time, and that begs the question: How many does it take?

R. Nachman: I taught you that the story itself may be redemptive. Turn it and turn it, it's yours now. Everything might be contained within the story.

Ibn Gabirol: We began in silence. We might end in silence too. And we might not.

Into your hands I entrust my spirit
At the time that I lie down and the time that I rise up
And with my spirit my body too
G*d is with me I shall not fear.

Letter

Waiting for you
Come toward
Angels of peace

Bless us
Toward peace
Angels of peace

When you leave
Leave toward peace
Angels of peace

Angels
Occupying sides
Warring over my soul

Third set of angels
Toward Peace
Reconcilation-ists

Angels of mercy
Malakhei ha-Rachamim
Middle pole

Welcome them
Integration-ists
Before peace

Mercy
Go toward peace
Long walk

Yours,
Holy and Blessed One

Maimonides Hafez Rumi Ibn Gabirol and James Baldwin Confer

All of them working
The repairs

From over the
Divide

They chose me to
Transcribe

On the subject of what
Constitutes

Whole
W-h-o-l-e

* * *

Maimonides taught
Keep it pure

When truth arises
Minimize surprises

Disorganization
Confusion distraction tenses

Build around the truth
With fences

Buttress guidelines and
Protection

Above all
Or-gan-i-za-tion

This is what I did
12th century

This will help
Even if it will not stand

You will be remembered for having
Planned

* * *

Shlomo son of Gabirol
Matter and form

In Muslim Spain adapting
Language poetry philosophy

I was universally
Dis-satisfied

Writing in Arabic
11th century

G*d the fountain of life
Through the river of return

We come back to
Source

Mystics claimed me from
"Yesod"

"Foundation" sentiment
Kabbalistic

Mystic sense premature
I was so insecure

Anti-social more specific
I fashioned a she-*golem* of wood

With a sweetheart
I may have been happier

But not more
prolific

                                    *   *   *

Hafez Persian
I am named for memorization

14th century
I knew Koran by heart

Listening to my Father's
Recitation

I knew all of
Rumi

In love with a beautiful
Unattainable woman

I drew a circle
Around myself

Forty days and forty nights
Vigil

*   *   *

Rumi
Balkhi

Mevlana/Mawlana
I am called our master

13th century
Settling into life at the

Madrassah until I met
Shams

Shams disappeared
Where should I seek?

I am the same as he
His essence speaks through me

I have been looking for
Myself

*   *   *

I have looked for guidance in
Wine

We might have thought
*G*d was there*

Roots of the roots
Of the Roots

There is I and there is
You

But not room for
Two

Knock knock who's there
You

*   *   *

You may come in since
You have cooked away

Your I
You are not a drop

In the Ocean
You are an ocean

In a drop
The universe in

Ecstatic
Motion

You will keep breaking your
Heart

Until it
Opens

* * *

James Baldwin dying
In 1987

Wholeness not
Our aspiration

Everything splintered
We fill the cracks in gold tincture

Beauty
Be bold

We may even
Give up the language of whole

* * *

Some of us make
Repairs

Some of us visioning
Beauty there

From our flaws
We build a menorah in the air

Above our heads
A vision

This light might illumine
Everywhere

What one person praises
Another person curses

We have fashioned a menorah
Out of flaws and verses

Now we begin
Its repair

Psalm 105:1-5

Hodu Find your gratitude
Kiru Say it out loud
Shiru Sing it swing it
Sichu Dia-logue it

Praise *Hit-ha-le-lu*
Use your mind *Dirshu*
Remember *Zikhru*

Halelu Halelu Halelu-Yah

Ki Zakhar et
D'var kodsho

Remember that
Holy Word

Ha-le-lu-Yah

—from the *Duke of Psalms*

תהילים ק"ה:א'-ה'

(א) הוֹדוּ לַיהוָה קִרְאוּ בִשְׁמוֹ הוֹדִיעוּ
בָעַמִּים עֲלִילוֹתָיו׃ (ב) שִׁירוּ־לוֹ
זַמְּרוּ־לוֹ שִׂיחוּ בְּכָל־נִפְלְאוֹתָיו׃ (ג)
הִתְהַלְלוּ בְּשֵׁם קָדְשׁוֹ יִשְׂמַח לֵב ׀
מְבַקְשֵׁי יְהוָה׃ (ד) דִּרְשׁוּ יְהוָה וְעֻזּוֹ
בַּקְּשׁוּ פָנָיו תָּמִיד׃ (ה) זִכְרוּ
נִפְלְאוֹתָיו אֲשֶׁר־עָשָׂה מֹפְתָיו
וּמִשְׁפְּטֵי־פִיו׃

www.ingramcontent.com/pod-product-compliance
Lightning Source LLC
Chambersburg PA
CBHW062115080426
42734CB00012B/2879